WORD OF THE YEAR

TRUE STORIES ABOUT INTENTIONAL LIVING USING THE POWER OF A SINGLE WORD

Dimple Mukherjee

Dimple Mukherjee
www.dimplemukherjee.com

Copyright © 2021 by Dimple Mukherjee.

Copy Editing: Jessica Willingham, jessicawillingham.com
Cover Design: Jessica Bramlett, jessicadesign.co

All rights reserved. No part of this publication may be reproduced, distributed or transmitted in any form or by any means, including photocopying, recording, or other electronic or mechanical methods, without the prior written permission of the publisher, except in the case of brief quotations embodied in critical reviews and certain other noncommercial uses permitted by copyright law. For permission requests, write to the author, at info@dimplemukherjee.com

The author of this book does not dispense medical advice or prescribe the use of any technique as a form of treatment for physical, emotional, or medical problems without the advice of a qualified health professional, either directly or indirectly. The intent of the author is to provide inspiration to help you create a fulfilling, meaningful, and joyful life. In the event you use any of the information in this book for yourself, the author and publisher assume no responsibility for your actions.

Dimple Mukherjee
www.dimplemukherjee.com

Word of the Year: True Stories About Intentional Living Using the Power of a Single Word/ Dimple Mukherjee. —1st ed.
Paperback ISBN 978-1-7779503-0-9

Word of the Year

CONTENTS

FOREWARD 6
WHAT'S IN A WORD 9
WORDS CREATE YOUR LIFE 14
LOVE: MANIFESTATION IN THE HIGHEST FORM 22
DEVOTED 31
EXPANSION 36
DELIGHT 40
PLAYFUL 43
FAITH 47
OPEN 51
SLOW 57
MAGIC 62
BALANCE 66
KEEP GOING 73
WORDS AS TRUTHS 79
READER REFLECTIONS 85
CLOSING 109
GRATITUDE 111

yourself, the author and publisher assume no responsibility for your actions.

Dimple Mukherjee
www.dimplemukherjee.com

Word of the Year: True Stories About Intentional Living Using the Power of a Single Word/ Dimple Mukherjee. —1st ed.
Paperback ISBN 978-1-7779503-0-9

CONTENTS

FOREWARD 6
WHAT'S IN A WORD 9
WORDS CREATE YOUR LIFE 14
LOVE: MANIFESTATION IN THE HIGHEST FORM 22
DEVOTED 31
EXPANSION 36
DELIGHT 40
PLAYFUL 43
FAITH 47
OPEN 51
SLOW 57
MAGIC 62
BALANCE 66
KEEP GOING 73
WORDS AS TRUTHS 79
READER REFLECTIONS 85
CLOSING 109
GRATITUDE 111

This book is dedicated to my parents, Ratna and Dayal Mirchandani, for teaching me that through hard work, humility and hope, anything is possible.

FOREWARD

Words weave magic. They are the anthems of freedom and joy that we belt out in our favorite summer song. They are the lingering memories of whispered adoration from a lover. They are the bones of our most private thoughts.

No matter who you are, where you live or how many years you've spent on this planet, your human experience has been drenched in a sea of words.

As an author and wordsmith, I am in awe of the invisible power they harness. For me they come through like little bursts of light and sound, a harmonic force that I immediately want to pair with another and another until they are singing with gusto. Strung together, they make sense of feelings I couldn't previously touch and give form to thoughts that once lived shapeless in my mind.

But perhaps most importantly, words are containers. And when paired with intention and emotion, they have the power to hold space and frequency for anyone who dares cast their spell. When activated, they are faithful companions and dutiful time-travelers laying the foundation for the life we want to live and the world we want to see.

I'm obviously a big fan of their work.

I began the practice of choosing a Word of the Year in 2007. You'll read more about my story later in the book, but suffice to say, I was enchanted by this idea that a single word could act as the container for my most intimate intentions and desires. A singular note, strummed over and over in the course of a year, reminding me of the song my soul craves to sing, and giving me a tune to return to when I wander off key...

Magic.

That practice has evolved for me as words have shown me more of their power. What once were intentions full of striving and force have softened into clearings for surrender and surprise. Words have shown me that, like water, we are most potent when we yield to the flow and gently point ourselves downstream.

The collection of stories in this book offers a chance for you too to find your connection to the power of words. When we share our stories, we share our magic, and woven in these words you will find spells of hope, possibility, joy, and love. Somewhere in these pages you will see yourself mirrored back to you, and hopefully in that moment you will realize how powerful you really are.

May your journey with words be intentional and loving, and may your years be full of moments that make your heart sing.

- Kayla Floyd, Award-Winning Author of *Wondrous You* and the poem "Words Have Power."

WHAT'S IN A WORD?

Think of a Word of the Year as your North Star — a word that you keep returning to in how you live your life, day after day. Someone once said to me, "I like the idea of my word being a spell." It took me all of a millisecond before I realized the magnitude of this sentence. That's exactly it isn't it? Your word does indeed cast a spell on you. From children's books to high-powered motivational conferences, naming what you desire is considered the first step to attaining success. Our words are ancient magic, capable of calling in the future.

I turned to Google. What does it mean to cast a spell? To my delight, this is what I found:

- to attract someone very strongly and to keep their attention completely
- to use magic words to change someone

Word of the Year

Skimming through all my words of the year — Love, Audacity, Flow, Spirit, Command, and Tend — I notice how quickly I'm dropping into memories created from these words. Moments I otherwise would struggle to recall and savor.

The real generosity here is that your Word of the Year is your guiding word, bringing you the gift of present moments *and* transcendence. When you choose a Word of the Year, you can cast a spell on your life.

As I turned to the chalkboard in my home office, nestled between my teak credenza and an overflowing mahogany bookcase, I scripted the word Flow with a fancy gold marker-chalk onto the dusty black background. Stepping back, I nodded my head in approval. Flow continued to feel good 24 hours after I called it in. Flow had captured my attention. From what I know now, the Call in Your Word practice has had a similar effect on many.

I presume that phonetics has something to do with it. Flow most definitely has a ring to it, don't you think? Akin to the sound of a newborn's cry at birth, lunchtime bells signaling recess, or laughter rippling throughout the house after a night's meal. Flow captivated me. My eyes glazed over the chalkboard once more as I stepped further back and repeated the word out loud as if to convince myself that Flow was it. This was the year I'd ensure my life was going to run smoothly and effortlessly. As I stepped out of my office that evening, a wave of contentment washed over me and I giggled to myself. It seemed I'd unknowingly made a secret pact with my Word of the Year and, despite feeling silly, I couldn't help but wonder how had I come to love this word so deeply already.

The next morning, I rushed into my office in a frenzy after realizing I was late for a client call. I didn't pay any attention to my chalkboard and sat down on my desk with my back to it as I frantically dialed the phone, rehearsing the apology I was about to make to my client for being five minutes late. Somewhere in my subconscious, I'm sure I cursed at Flow in that moment. What I was experiencing was anything but that.

By the time my client call had ended, my racing heart had returned to its normal rhythm and my client was completely understanding. She informed me that because I was late to the call, she had managed to spend the extra five minutes on deep breathing, which allowed her to be calmer for our call together. As I stood up to stretch, I noticed extra writing on my chalkboard. Sometime last night, my then 10-year-old took it upon himself to add a few words to Flow.

My chalkboard read: *Go with the* Flow.

That's when I knew that a word can take on a life of its own and most definitely leave you spellbound.

As you read through these pages, I hope that's exactly how you'll feel. There's something magical and exciting about all the possibilities that can be conjured by a single word. With each story, I hope you feel drawn in and captivated. With each experience, I hope you're enchanted. I hope you're as mesmerized by these beautiful individuals as I was, and you're inspired by these deep conversations to use your words to catapult into creating meaningful connections.

Most of all, I hope you'll revisit your dreams and desires as you read through the words in this tiny book and cultivate a fulfilling life, one word at a time.

xo

Dimple

WORDS CREATE YOUR LIFE

My usual weekly trip to the natural health food store felt different on that day. I lingered along the book aisle much longer than I had anticipated while the smells of botanicals permeated my body, calming me as I turned the crisp pages of a newly-released lifestyle cookbook. This health store was a haven, an escape from the prison that was my home, the loosening and tattered threads of my marriage, and the intolerable sounds of kids who were just being as they should be. It never occurred to me that the even the simplest of imbalances were noxious to my nervous system. That's how broken I was.

I made my way to the cashier to pay for some very expensive supplements prescribed by my naturopath and decided to put down the cookbook next to them. So typical of me. I'm always trying to do the "right thing." Maybe this would be the answer to the falling pieces of my life.

Perhaps this lifestyle cookbook could teach me how to take the first step in the right direction. The optimist in me dreamt about a better outcome. If only I could heal, all else would fall into place.

As I read this book, I became engrossed in the author's journey through cancer and the various ways she overcame a rare health condition that had her on her knees. Admiring her grit and resiliency, I did what I always do when I read the stories of humans that impress me: I started to idolize her. I put her on a pedestal and became obsessed with her blogs, newsletters, and social media presence. I wanted to be her. I spent much more time in her life than I did in mine, and now that I've had time to reflect on it, it's clear that other people's makeover stories felt much sexier to me than my own. Yes, they were inspirational but the inspiration didn't get me far. These stories became welcomed distractions to the life I didn't want to live.

At the time, the online world was starting to boom and I found myself gravitating toward stories and more stories of women who had turned their lives around after adversities. Within a matter of days from the time I picked up this one book at my local health store, I became lost in a sea of endless stories of many incredible women. My thirst for these stories was unquenchable. Clicking through the colorful websites, I stumbled upon a woman whose writing felt like a warm vanilla-colored cashmere blanket against my own lightly-tanned skin on a cool, crisp autumn morning. I melted into her words over and over again. It was in those initial days and weeks of scrolling her pastel shades of divine and glorious pages when I realized how words have the power to change lives. Little did I know that her words would harbor in my body for years to come.

Her words became my truth. I found myself in her words over and over again. She said all the things that I felt into the depth of my core but couldn't articulate. Imagine my joy when I mustered up the courage to join one of her online programs, even though my inner critic had lots to say about why I couldn't afford it. This was the start of a new addiction, a new vice for me. These online spaces became my home and gave me solace. In clicking the "join" links, I was allowed to hope for something new and it felt like a promise of better things. And one day, it was.

About seven years ago or so, when the world was busy baking delightful Christmas treats and sipping on hot cocoa while gathered around a simmering fire or invading the chaotic malls for some last-minute shopping, I was scrolling through my email inbox in the quiet of my home. After years of unhappy holidays, I had learned the hard way — I knew that being at home for the holidays was the best place to be, surrounded by the simplicity of good food, good wine, and laughter. If I needed a dose of merry, I'd ask Siri to play "Jingle Bells" by Diana Krall in the background while I pulled out my iPad to explore how others were going to celebrate the end of another year. Cuddled up on my favourite arm chair in the wee hours of the morning, with my hands wrapped around a cup of steaming hot coffee, I sunk into the emails that I saved exactly for moments like this — my daily dose of hygge.

And there it was. Embedded in my emails of last minute shopping flash sales, promotions, and a new yoga class recording was a subject line that read "Word of the Year" from my favorite blogger. She was at it again, and this time I was especially curious. A Word of the Year sounded intriguing and my eyes lit up as I eagerly clicked the newsletter link. I barely got through the first paragraph and I was hooked. When you know, you just know. I signed up for a five-day "Find Your Word of the Year" experience. While I was still not fully clear on what I was getting into, I knew I felt magic in the air.

Some things are just like that. That December morning, I stepped into a space where I was willing to be surprised. I was willing to surrender, and I was willing to believe. It was a new and exciting way of being. It reminded me of my childlike wonder and how alive I used to feel in that energy. The possibilities were all for me to sink into and packaged into the promise of one word. I had permission to hold onto that word as one would a treasure. To coddle it, to be in awe of it, and to hold it in high regard for as long as I needed to. In doing so, I would be honoring the truest parts of myself.

Imagining myself into my word the first year was a sacred act and one that I've kept close to my heart since. The longing for a word at the start of each new year is as innate as dreaming and desiring for more — more out of me and more out of my life. My word anchors me during the toughest of times with its whispers of encouragement and hope. My word steps back to give me space to ponder over choices but never strays out of reach, and is the first to celebrate with me when triumphs, big or small, cross my path. In times of darkness, my word is a much-needed resting station as I nestle into its embrace with my woes and fears only to be reminded that this too shall pass. It creates a depth of longing that otherwise would be left unseen and unheard, like a hidden passage that no one knows about, yet fully exists. Discovering my word would mean leaving behind the old and worn paths to enter the lightly treaded and unfamiliar ones. My word tempts me, as it should. It nudges me to reach for that which I don't feel I deserve and reminds me that this one precious life, as Mary Oliver would say, is mine for the taking. Unequivocally, my word is telling me that it can be anything I want it to be, anything I need it to be. It drowns out the noise that tells me otherwise.

In a way, I've held onto my word for dear life because it's how life should be, dear.

There comes a time when defining moments change the trajectory of your life. For me, one of those moments was that day in the health store in 2010, when something as simple as stumbling upon the inspirational and heartbreaking story of an author became the energy source for me to seek out my own truth and to create something out of it. It led me to the energy of a simple and powerful practice, to formalize it so that I could easily share it, and most importantly, to cultivate a rich community. I believe that by harnessing the energy of a like-minded community, you can go so much further than you would alone. I can't think of a better way to do that than through storytelling. It's why I love bringing value-oriented and purposeful individuals together over the Word of the Year and the Call in Your Word Practice. While the Word of the Year can shape your next 12 months, the Call in Your Word practice is yours for the taking whenever the time is right for you. I have thoroughly enjoyed creating the online Call in Your Word program, the Call in Your Word annual workshops, and the yearlong Live Your Word community and coaching program. All of these have been a labor of love and a practice that I commit to building upon.

For now, I'm coming alive by telling stories, one word at a time. Just as I fell down the rabbit hole of uplifting and inspiring stories, my intention with this book is to pay it forward and give another woman a soft spot to land within herself. The following are 11 stories of women being guided by a single word, and how unleashing the divine inner wisdom can have tremendous ripples.

LOVE: MANIFESTATION IN THE HIGHEST FORM

It was December 2015 when I called in Love as my word for 2016. I secretly thought to myself, maybe this will finally be the year I'll fall in love with myself.

It was early January 2016 when I walked into a new therapist's office and made my claim. "I'm here to see you because I need support to leave a toxic relationship that I haven't managed to let go of," I told her. The pain that sat in the pit of my stomach was deep and strong. I could still taste the acidity on my tongue, feel the dried up and patchy tears under my eyes from days of bawling, hear the ringing of loud voices, screams, and banging doors, see his bloodshot eyes staring back at me — the kind of redness that only came with years of drug abuse. I could still sense his gripping hands around my neck as he forcefully pushed me against the cold, barren walls of a stairwell. Years of unreconciled pain still burned like fire in my gut.

How I came up with that bold ask in the therapist's office on a dull and dreary winter's day is beyond me. I was desperate. I was so desperate for help because I no longer trusted my heart to take care of me, as she bloody well should have all these years. I said it and then stared off into the distance, lost in pain and regret.

"Dimple," called out my therapist in her soothing British accent, bringing me back into the little room that enveloped us. Sitting across from her, I immediately felt some relief and knew that everything would eventually be alright, but it wasn't going to be easy. Her gentle firmness and the wrinkled lines of wisdom around the corners of her eyes told me so. A low-rise wooden bookshelf to my right beckoned. Titles like "How to Be an Adult in a Relationship," "Hold Me Tight," and "Loving Bravely" were taunting and teasing, reminding me of how horribly I'd failed in life, and all the years lost in haunting relationships.

...

The ensuing months did not bring about a piercing heartbreak as I had thought it would. I imagine it was because I'd dissociated from this relationship long before I knew I had. The countless nights of crying while lying alone in bed, the infinite scrolling through steamy texts between him and other women, and the recurring discoveries of small bags of cocaine in his dresser drawer had left me empty and devoid. By this point, I was completely numb to pain. These days, time and place were an illusion. I was never sure where I was waking up, or what I was awakening to.

This inner struggle and the desire to feel free prompted me to seek out books, courses, and workshops that would continue to convince me that self-love was the only way to healthy love. I knew it was the answer, but what was the block? Why was I still failing in relationships after years of this? Why was I still yearning for emotionally unavailable men? And why did I even try to justify that this time, it'll be different?

While I explored the terrain of casual mating, I also had the best date of my life. A self-love program challenged me to take myself on a date. The idea of taking myself out started as a seed and then sprouted into a stunning little flower. I prepped for a date with myself in February, just at the cusp of Valentine's Day. I passed up a night at home with a mind-blowing meal, a bottle of red on the couch, and a few episodes of mindless TV and braved a night out on the town — totally alone. Before leaving home to a reserved table for one at a fine Italian bistro, I took some time to meditate and visualize how I wanted the night to go and drove to the restaurant. I was seated at the chef's table.

Truth be told, I felt uncomfortable for a handful of short-lived seconds. The chefs were warm, funny, and showed me a level of hospitality that totally induced the warm and fuzzies. People are so generous when you give them a chance, you know? Not only did I pick up a few cooking skills by sitting where the action was, but I was thoroughly pampered by the chefs with tons of food tastings, free wine, rich conversations, and an incredible array of desserts to end the night on a high note. I had one of the best dates I've ever had.

By June, my ex still hadn't completely left my life. A truth I hated admitting, but I was solid in my decision of never returning to him and told him so. My conscience was clear. Yet he insisted on showing up. At my doorstep, in my inbox, and through voicemails. He often spoke of leaving the city and I awaited his departure with great anticipation.

As I continued to lengthen the distance between him and me, I attended a vision board workshop in September 2016. Images of words like passion, humor, romance, love, and more filled the upper right quadrant of my board. That was the section I had reserved especially for love. I wanted someone who had all these qualities and more. Why not? I managed to convince myself that I deserved love. Clipping through magazines, the headline caught my eye: "Crash a wedding with a stranger." I stuck it on my vision board. It reminded me of fun — something I hadn't had in a long while. It'd be so fun to have a partner who was also playful.

My ex finally left the city on October 21, 2016. I flew out to San Francisco the following day for a much-needed vacation with my two older sons. We explored Fisherman's Wharf, Napa Valley wineries, crooked Lombard Street, a 49ers game, Ghirardelli Chocolate Company, Carmel-by- the-Sea, Sausalito, and more. After a fun-filled week of adventure, I was desperately craving some alone time. That meant a few hours to myself in a tight seat under fluorescent lights on the plane ride back home. Despite a delight of a trip, there were moments of deep ache over the loss of my 8-year relationship as I lay alone at night in a strange city far away from home. Unfamiliarity had a way of pulling out the grief that I was working so hard on burying. Searching for a way to release some of the lingering grief, I grabbed my bright red journal from my carry-on bag just as the fasten seat belt signs came on.

My journaling was disrupted throughout the flight in between credit card requests to buy food and drinks off the flight attendant's trolley and the never-ending questions around the length of the plane ride, dinner plans, and who is picking us up when we land. Finally, the two boys passed out shortly before landing and I returned to the page feeling fully ready. Ready to date myself, and someone else. We were now into the end of October and throughout the year I had promised myself that I wouldn't sign on to any dating apps because I just wasn't ready. I convinced myself that I had to be alone to take a break from all the men I had been with since I was 18. I was shocked to realize I hadn't been single during all my adult years. I wrote callously in my journal that 10 months of being "alone" was good enough. I felt excited and had a sudden urge to write a letter to the universe requesting the man of my dreams. No sooner had my pen hit the paper when I heard, "Cabin crew. Prepare for landing."

Dear Universe. And then I dared to ask. I wrote feverishly as I listed all the brilliant qualities anyone could ever desire in a partner. Why not? For the first time in my life, I felt like I deserved it. It didn't even occur to me how one man could possibly be all those things. I forgot about my vision board in that moment. Clearly, these desires were deep within me. I admit it was a generous wish list. Being calculative, I thought if I asked for it all, I may just be lucky enough to receive most. Signing off *Love, Dimple* just as the wheels of the airplane hit the landing pad of the Toronto Pearson Airport felt serendipitous. We'd arrived and I was ready to date. Reaching for my phone, I turned it on in anticipation of all the messages and calls I must have missed while airborne. One by one, they started to trickle in. After scrolling through my WhatsApp messages, I turned to my texts. "Hey are you back from Cali?" wrote a man who I'd loosely call a friend, and a friend who almost never texted me.

I found myself at an epic party that same night with the man who almost never texted me. As we chatted, he delicately danced around my relationship status. When he heard that I had ended it this time for sure, he breathed a sigh of relief and we returned to our conversation with an element of closeness that we've never shared before. What came next is somewhat of an enigma. I can't remember what lead us to this point, perhaps divine intervention. When he asked, "Wouldn't it be so fun if we crashed a wedding together?" I was instantly transported to the love corner of my vision board. *There is no way this man is THE man*, I repeated in my mind as I had a private conversation with source, higher self, the universe. I was convinced that my vision board and my letter to the universe had failed me because the man sitting in front of me was someone I'd joke around with and felt comfortable enough to be myself with. I just didn't think of him that way.

On December 26, 2016, four days before the end of the year, someone that I would've never seen myself with before confessed that he loved me over a George Michael playlist, crackling fireplace, and few glasses of red. Ending the year with the word Love by my side, I reflected on how I managed to get rid of toxic love, cultivate self-love, and fall in love in 2016. Love has been one of my most magnificent words of the year.

DEVOTED

"I like the idea of the word being a spell."

Stephanie shared with me that she became attracted to the practice of Call in Your Word in 2013 when she was in her last year of her university. She had been following a scrapbooker/blogger who would write about the "one little word" and was hooked. Stephanie hasn't looked back since.

Over the years, I've seen Stephanie in her true element as a creative consultant for small business owners and entrepreneurs. She's reflected with me deeply and intentionally about this practice. Our conversation was super rich and we both walked away from it feeling deeply grateful for the opportunity to discuss the goodness of what this practice has to offer so many of us!

Remember earlier in the book I mentioned that someone once said to me, "I like the idea of the word being a spell." Exact quote by Stephanie. She recalled that one of her most potent word over the years has been Abundance. Even though she hadn't quite lived her word as intentionally as she had with her words in the past, Abundance showed up for her strongly. She embodied the energy of Abundance and its energy. In short, this practice does not disappoint. According to Stephanie, the Word of the Year practice is "playful, fun and whimsical!" Note to self: Whimsy or Whimsical will have to be my word sometime soon! I just love the way this word instantly lights me up.

Stephanie had more to say about the value of calling in and living your word. "My word allows me to process and analyze my world better and provides for richer and more valuable experiences," she said. In other words, it adds a layer of depth — a depth to self and to others. "My close friend also chooses a word and it makes this experience with her that much better. To be witnessed is a gift. I get a lot of inspiration from other people's words." Looking at the world through the lens of other people's words has quickly become one of Stephanie's favorite ways of engaging in this practice.

When I asked Stephanie who she would be without this practice, she said "the years would blend in together a lot more." Words give the years clarity and distinctions. They provide an element of anchoring, connecting the dots, and tying the stories together.

But here's the catch. Stephanie taught me that when you call in your word, you're also calling in its opposite. Like all conscious desires, a word also carries a shadow. If your Word of the Year is Celebrate, you might call in opportunities to experience more joy *and* plenty of examples of instances, people, and events in your life that are unworthy of celebration. Since you chose Celebration as your word and intention, you have the chance to lean into moments of joy, while recognizing and ridding yourself of what does not align with your word. That's hard work! While this practice can be light and fun, it can also provide alternative perspectives – ones you might never have considered.

When calling in a Word of the Year, Stephanie typically engages in a reflection process, usually in the form of journaling. She may utilize prompts or write freely. Once she has narrowed her options down to a few words, she will "test" them with trusted friends to gain valuable insights.

After she has called in a Word of the Year, Stephanie fully embraces and lives her word as intentionally as she can. She starts off by writing a blog post about her word. Sometimes she will write a second blog post later in the year with an update on how her word is manifesting. Stephanie has been known to create a personalized hashtag or two using her Word of the Year. In the past year, Stephanie gifted herself a talisman – a gorgeous ring to symbolize her word. Being an avid reader, Stephanie found a book that aligned with her Word of the Year, Devoted. The book was aptly named "Devotions: The Selected Poems of Mary Oliver."

Stephanie and I chatted about Devoted, her word for 2020. She called in this word with the intention of exercising self-care in a way that felt more meaningful. She chose the word Devoted over Self-Care because Devoted had more depth for her. Devoted also denoted timelessness with an air of being non-negotiable. Stephanie pays attention to the energy of her words and seeks a more active word rather than a passive word. The act of Devotion, being Devoted, felt like an active word.

At the end of it all, Devoted brought humility into Stephanie's life. In the wake of the pandemic year of 2020, Devoted revealed the purity in the every day which has been a humbling experience for Stephanie.

EXPANSION

"You find the opposite of your word and start shrinking away from it."

Julia loves bringing people together to honor self-care in workshops, events, and retreats. When Julia and I chatted, the first thing she said to me was: "I'm a fan of living my life one word at a time." She paused, then said, "Admittedly, I haven't made this a consistent practice yet."

The first time she came across the practice was in 2013. She was introduced to it by a colleague and felt herself resonating with it. Soon, another friend offered her a Word of the Year prompt, and Julia was hooked. She reflected, "I just had to be invited."

The next year, Julia walked the Camino. She committed to walking 25 kilometers per day over five weeks. A true dedication to her inner strength, Julia had called in Discipline as her Word of the Year for 2014 with the knowing that she can do hard things.

Fast forward to this year and Julia didn't have an opportunity to engage in a formal process. "My word chose me," she said. Julia's word for 2021 is Expansion. She noticed the word Expand kept showing up — during a psychic reading, while reading a book ("The word just jumped off the page!") and in conversation with her mother. Julia found that Expansion has been lending itself to growth and community.

Her experiences with the Word of the Year practice have been fulfilling and enriching for Julia. She explained that the most rewarding aspect of the practice is "having a framework to invite desired experiences into existence." In other words (pun not intended!), being able to co-create a life she wants with her guiding word has helped her evolve and navigate muddy waters to get to the other side. Julia reflected on how her word has been her guidepost – "it keeps bringing you back to what is important." Her word is a quick and poignant reminder of what to focus on and what to let go. Julia has also noticed, as many do who engage in this practice, that her words beckon synchronicities. Things start to happen. Good things. "When you are aware of something, you see more of it," Julia said. "In that moment, you are cultivating magic. What you focus on grows and I really believe in that. Even today, I was writing a post on unfurling and it has Expansion energy all over it."

Do you know what else happens? "You find the opposite of your word and start shrinking away from it." Finding clarity is one of the greatest gifts of this practice.

Some years, Julia's process of calling in a word is formalized, and other years, not so much. During the year of Discipline, Julia recalled that she journaled and chatted with friends and colleagues about her word so that she could hold herself true to her word. She even drew her word and took a photo of it. Other years, the words have found her.

Julia's favorite part of this practice is the connections that form because of it. "Once you have a word, it's something you want to talk about. I would definitely stop and share my experiences with people if I heard my word pop up in their conversation. When others witness you in your word and reflect it back to you, you feel seen and heard." Her enthusiasm was palpable.

Going forward, Julia is curious to hear more stories about how words have unfolded for others.

DELIGHT

"The juxtaposition between my word and the state of our world in the midst of a pandemic is medicinal."

A creative woman after my own heart, Sonja is a culinarian extraordinaire. She is the founder of Nurture. Nurture creates intentional spaces of community, connection, and nourishment. The coming together over good food and good company is how I see Sonja. Her gifts are many and her talents are diverse. I couldn't wait to jump on a call with Sonja to hear about her Call in Your Word process.

Sonja has been calling in a Word of the Year for the past six years. She noticed it when fellow Pinterest or Instagram members started posting their words. But it wasn't until her friend, Stephanie (yes, the very same Stephanie mentioned earlier in the book) nudged her towards this practice that inspired Sonja to solidify her own.

Words have always been a part of Sonja's life. "I pay attention, a lot of attention, to words," she said. Very much a wordsmith herself, Sonja listens to the wisdom of her body when she calls in a word. The chosen word has to resonate viscerally — it's Sonja's litmus test. Not one to loosely engage in any practice, Sonja consults with a thesaurus to gather more synonyms for words she is considering. If the mood strikes, she might consider speaking to others about her choices.

Sonja called in Delight as her Word of the Year in 2020. She played with a few words, waiting and seeking for signs that would lead her to her word. "I kept hearing over and over again that I needed play and joy in my life," she said. "People would tell me that I was too serious. A few words came before Delight but they didn't resonate with me. When Delight came up, I felt it in my body. It was a strong sensation."

Word of the Year

Sonja shared with me in October of 2020 that it was quite a funny year for her word. Somehow the pandemic and Delight did not seem to fit together. But Sonja found a meaning behind it all. "The juxtaposition between my word and the state of our world in the midst of a pandemic is medicinal in a way," reflected Sonja. I love how Sonja found the light in the dark with her word. Her intention for Delight was to notice the delight, to embody the delight.

And embody she did. Sonja was reminded by a dear friend to turn to Delight when things got tough and to shift through it all. Imagine?! Problem-solving your way through life's challenges with Delight by your side? What would be possible?

Sonja found mysticism in her word. "When I see Delight, I'm reminded that my life has meaning. I'm on the right path," she said. "The words have added to my life...they are my touchstone, a compass, a tool in my toolbox. They connect me to the divine."

PLAYFUL

"I enjoy surrendering to what may be with my word. The possibilities are endless and I'm happy to let them unfold as they will."

Call in a Your Word is a new practice for Georgia. She stumbled upon this practice mid-year in 2020 as a result of our paths crossing. Georgia joined the Live Your Word community in June 2020. The Live Your Word community was created by me and is a coming together of like-minded individuals who are simply in love with their words and want to live them to their full potential. Forever curious and a lifelong learner, Georgia was open to a new way of living intentionally with a word by her side. She was intrigued.

Even before our call in June 2020, Georgia knew her Word of the Year was Playful. She felt her word and didn't need me to coach her through this process. When I asked her how her word had been showing up for her, Georgia said, "It hasn't shown up for me as I planned it. The last couple of years, I've been pretty serious and I needed a permission slip to be less serious. To me, play translates into laughter, color, and feeling into the different and quirky sides of people. When you play, that's what happens." Georgia said she wanted to "set the stage, lay the groundwork" for the year ahead with Playful by her side. She desired connection with others through play, storytelling, laughter, and daydreaming while being heart-centered. Playful felt like all of that and more.

From June until December 2020, Georgia showed up to the Live Your Word community fully, gathering with other courageous women who valued intentional living. Georgia started meditation and would use Post-it notes as her permission slips to be Playful. She found that Playful helped her make decisions more authentically and she invited in more opportunities for play. Over time, Georgia also noticed that Playful gave her permission to detach herself from outcomes and in her words, "not to overthink things" and ultimately allow herself to breathe a bit deeper and be more at ease. In just three months after calling in her word, Georgia shared that Playful had a message for her and it was to *slow down*. Georgia elaborated and came up with a brilliant insight: "slow is smooth and smooth is fast." Right? It's so true!

So, you may be surprised to hear that by the end of the year, Georgia recognized how her word had transformed to serve her best. "I don't think I've been super Playful this year but my word has definitely been my anchor and a tether," she said. "If I had not had the word Playful, my year would have been more intense because it certainly had the potential to be."

Inspired by her journey with Playful, Georgia continues to call in a Word of the Year. Her word for 2021 is Whole. "I want to walk away feeling more full, more enriched, more comfortable, and with less questioning," she said. In a way, Whole is a natural sequel to Playful.

Word of the Year

When Georgia reflected on the practice of Call in Your Word, she found that she enjoys surrendering to what may come with her word. The possibilities are endless and she is happy to let them unfold as they will.

FAITH

"The woven aspect of this practice and this tool is different from therapy. While somatic therapy shakes my body, my word gifts me the depth without the heaviness. My word carries with it a lighter frequency that I can't access in therapy."

Meeting R.G. was an act of synchronicity. I was surprised when she messaged me one day to inquire about the Live Your Word community. For the record, I adore heartfelt and sincere messages from people whom I've never met and the energetic connections that are created in the space between us. It's exactly how I felt about R.G. as soon as we met online. She felt like someone I'd known for a long time and not like a stranger I was about to dig deep and fast with. It was easy for me to do that with R.G. because besides being a clinical counselor, R.G. walked her talk. She is no stranger to the depth of personal work.

R.G.'s word for 2021 is Faith. When I asked R.G. what drew her to the practice of Call in Your Word, she said, "I feel like the word was already in me but there was a desire for clarity. The coolest part about it is that it was in my subconscious and the actual practice offers life to the spirit of the word. It calls it out. It awakens it." R.G. has had a long-term relationship with Faith, but it was only this year that her word decided to take it to the next level.

Faith provided R.G. with a protective layer. R.G. is not one for small talk and she has found that with the support of Faith, she has been able to find the courage to dive deeper into conversations with others and to be vulnerable. R.G. joined the Live Your Word community in May 2021. She has been such a valuable and deeply loved member of this community.

"Faith has gifted me a sense of grounding, working with the roots of my tree…when the wind blows, they don't lift." Faith has been R.G.'s anchor (there is anchor again!) and helped her find acceptance. R.G. has also been dancing with the different variations of Faith. Most recently she stumbled upon "quiet Faith"— the type of Faith that has been urging her to sit in silence and to be with her breath. I remember these words of R.G. very clearly one Sunday morning during our monthly Live Your Word gatherings. She shared "depth invited me to see where Faith was and Faith allowed me to get depth." It's in moments like these when I'm reminded of why this practice has been a beacon of light for many.

What R.G. has appreciated the most about calling in and living her word is the ease with which it has integrated into her life. "The word becomes woven into your awareness," she said. "It is much more effortless than having a daily reminder which is yet another thing you have to remember. Your word is respectful of your boundaries. It does not force. It's natural. It's easy." If she didn't have access to this practice, R.G. believes that trauma would have lifted her away from her roots. "I would have been in chaos much longer and I would have been much more reactive. I don't like being in a reactive state. This practice has brought me closer to my essence faster and this is very important to me."

As a clinical professional, R.G. has been surprised by the therapeutic power of the Call in Your Word practice. "The woven aspect of this practice and this tool is different from therapy," she explained. "While somatic therapy shakes my body, my word gifts me the depth without the heaviness. My word carries with it a lighter frequency that I can't access in therapy."

What does R.G. have to share with you about the Call in Your Word practice? "This is the kind of practice that can support an individual within a collective to bring focus and attention to your inner knowing," she said. "Your inner knowing is a seedling which you begin to nurture, water, and get to know as you deepen your connection with your word."

OPEN

"Your practice with your Word of the Year will gift you insights into untapped facets of yourself and allow you to move forward in an expansive way."

A dear friend and a lifelong supporter of all my ideas and creations, let's call her Mira, and I go way back. Growing up together, we've been through our shares of twists and turns in this mystical and ever-surprising journey called life. It came as no surprise that when I had wanted to celebrate the end of a year with my closest girlfriends, Mira was all in that one December night in 2015. My intention for the night was for us to hold each other in this magical space before the New Year so that we could co-create our lives and invite in the year ahead with our guiding words.

We haven't looked back since.

Word of the Year

Our Call in Your Word end-of-the-year party has become a favorite annual tradition. We look forward to check-ins, group chats, and inspirations when we feel less than enough throughout the year. We've witnessed each other's dreams come to fruition as we continue to gather, share and connect, reminding each other of how much power there is in setting our intentions in such a playful and fun manner.

Mira's most memorable word to date has been her word for 2017, Open. Wait till you hear her story but first, it's important to fill you in with a background because Mira's story is a tender one.

In 2015, Mira made a conscious decision to plan for another child. She called in Patience as her word for 2016. This word was multifaceted and had many layers to it. Most of all, it was calling upon her to be patient as she managed all the intricate complexities of this decision. She was up for the challenge.

Fast forward to the end of 2016 and Mira was not pregnant. She walked into the Call in Your Word party with us in December 2016 with full intention to keep it all together and to join in on the festivities even though she was breaking inside. When we pulled out the Tarot deck to evoke our words, Mira broke open. Mira recalled this moment perfectly. "I picked up the fertility card that night and wondered why did I pick this card?" It forced her to shift her mindset to possibilities and alternatives she hadn't considered. Mira dug deep within herself and shared her fertility challenges – and her difficulty coping.

As the night progressed, we doodled and journaled our way through our potential words with stickers, markers, sparkles, and the works – yeah, we go all out! Mira landed on Open. "Open just came to me. I told myself all will be okay. I will do my best. And I'll be Open to being pregnant or not."

From January until May 2017, Mira underwent in vitro fertilization, or I.V.F. She shared the following with me as she distinctly pulled out details from the past.

"I remember the process. It was very invasive and I hated the injections. I was mentally and physically exhausted. Open became a mantra. I kept telling myself to be Open to this because if I'm not Open to I.V.F., I won't conceive."

In May of 2017, Mira had had enough of the I.V.F. She had to try a new way to be Open. Open allowed her to pick herself up and to reclaim her life. She believed in herself and in her body. Mira told herself:

"I will be ok with my family exactly the way it is right now, in this moment."

"I am a strong woman."

"I am exactly where I need to be."

"To be honest, it took me some time to adjust, to accept, and to surrender to what was," Mira told me as I listened in awe to this beautiful woman before me. She was the epitome of courage, softness, and self-love rolled into one.

By May, Mira felt freedom. In August of 2017, she was pregnant. Even as she recounted the details of that day four years later in her interview with me, the excitement was palpable. "I was floored," she told me. "I was six weeks pregnant, full of emotions and also in shock. But once I was able to collect myself and had had a chance to reflect, I realized that when I released my limiting beliefs and treated myself with self-compassion, and gave myself permission to just be, my body could do what she needed to do. With my word Open, I arrived at...you are good enough." Some powerful words right there, don't you think?

Needless to say, Mira is a big fan of the Call in Your Word practice. Her favorite part about this practice is engaging in the end of the year Call in Your Word guided workshops (hosted by yours truly!) "There's a spark during our time together," Mira said. "You can sense the magic in the air that is exhilarating, exciting, and safe. It's just one of those nights when you can truly step in and sink deep within yourself while being held in community. That vibe is just something else!"

What Mira wants you to know about the Call in Your Word practice is that it will gift you insights into untapped facets of yourself and allow you to move forward in an expansive way. Without her word, Mira knows that she wouldn't be as mindful with her life as she has been in recent years. Her ability to reflect rather than to react impulsively to situations has been a change that she's been able to make with the support of her word.

SLOW

"A big part of this is the intuitive process of feeling into it, dropping into my body, looking at areas that I may have struggled with, and asking myself, where is the pull? A word that feels like a balm to that experience and feels soothing in response to my previous struggles will naturally become my word."

I met Nicole online. We belong to the same mastermind group of creative entrepreneurs who live with intention, so it came as no surprise to me that Nicole had been living her life one word at a time. I was curious to hear all about Nicole's experiences with this practice and her discoveries along the way. Being a visual artist and a creative mindfulness facilitator, Nicole knew a thing or two about being in the here and now.

"A friend of mine introduced me to this practice on a New Year's Eve about six years ago," Nicole said. "I was thinking of my intentions, a key word, a statement because my brain is creative and it loves clarity. It's calming for my nervous system to have a goal, a purpose." Nicole is often tempted to call in more than one word, and switches up her words a few times during the year. It feels right for her to align her words with what's happening in her life seasonally.

When calling in word, Nicole turns to the wisdom of her body. "A big part of this is the intuitive process – feeling into it, dropping into my body, looking at areas that I may have struggled with, and asking myself, where is the pull? A word that feels like a balm to that experience and feels soothing in response to my previous struggles will naturally become my word."

Truthfully, Nicole admitted that some years she's been more aware of her word in comparison to other years but for the past three years, calling in and living her Word of the Year has been a consistent practice for her. What has helped her live her word is visual cues. Nicole creates beautiful print series which then become visual manifestations of her words and sometimes threads of her previous words will also appear in her prints. For Nicole, conscious engagement in the visual process is essential to embodying the word. Nicole also loves to meet with a friend regularly, pull some animal spirit cards from an oracle deck and discuss their words of the year (definitely one of my favorite ways to breathe some life into my Word of the Year). Nicole reflected that a visual process "allows us to catch up in a really organic way."

What Nicole absolutely loves about this practice is how her word assumes the role of a North Star. "Whenever I have to make a complex decision, I ask myself, does this decision honor my word? It feels very powerful." Her word helps her navigate decisions.

For 2021, Nicole called in Slow as her Word of the Year. As unconventional as Nicole is with this practice and someone who definitely dances to her own beat, she confessed that she prefers to call in her word sometime during the fall season rather than at the end of the year. Fall, in a way, is a beginning. The colors are vibrant and a vivid reminder that change is the only constant. "There is a contrast in the energy of fall that feels fresh and new," she said.

Nicole came up with the term "grounded momentum" some time ago and this term led her to Slow. "I tend to step into a productive cycle in a way that I'm running on fumes and it feels great because I'm full of adrenaline but the downside of it is that I can really burn out," she said. "The concept of grounded momentum still has me moving forward but in a much more sustainable, somatic, and grounded in my body kind of way. It reminds me I have feet."

During the global lockdown, Slow allowed Nicole to change her expectations of what's possible while working and parenting from home full time. It was a time of simplifying and slowing the speed. Ironically, it was also in the year of Slow that Nicole launched her print series. The series was born out of Post-it notes. Slow allowed her to sink deep into this project with a sense of ease.

I love how Nicole's creative process mirrors her experiences with her word.

"I can't even not have a word anymore now that I've done it," Nicole shared at the end of our time together. "My word comes in and out of my consciousness and when I come back to it, it's always there, kind of like a good friend. This practice has a maternal energy to it. The word is, both, holding space and creating a container of focus for you. It allows you to be creative with the world around you. It's a very magical experience."

MAGIC

"The power of the Call in Your Word practice is in its simplicity."

Maria's work and way with plants, florals, and medicine grabbed my attention instantly. She's an artist and feng shui practitioner. As someone who delights in nature, I can fully appreciate Maria's love for her word for 2021: Magic. But before I get carried away with Magic (as easily as I do!), let's get cozy with Maria and her relationship with the practice of Call in Your Word.

Maria recalled that she started to call in a word three or four years ago but couldn't remember how this all came to fruition. She wondered if she'd heard about it on a podcast? Possibly. She'd heard somewhere that having a Word of the Year was a great alternative to setting New Year's resolutions and thought she'd give it a go. Since then, Maria has called in Radiance, Strength, and Community as her words. I was visualizing her nodding through the phone call as she exclaimed, "I like how my word is top of mind in many facets of my life."

When asked about how she calls in and lives her word, Maria said, "I just think about it. I don't have a formal practice. The word just comes to me and once I've conjured up my word, I mostly let my word unfold organically. I also journal on it and have a visual of it in my office."

Maria explained that her definition of Magic is "being willing to see things differently than they first appear and trusting the unseen even though I might not have tangible proof for them." Maria wanted to approach life in playful and expansive ways. She also asked herself: "How can I be delighted by the world around me in magical ways? How can I invite an element of awe?"

Maria's highlights with Magic have been many. "There is an aspect of things falling into place with more ease and less resistance," she said. "I've also gotten better at trusting my intuition and it has been guiding me with decision making. Intuition is what leads me to experience Magic. The more I trust that, the more Magic unfolds. My body feels happy, light, and sparkly when Magic is front and center." She also highlighted that "I feel Magic in my creative artistic practices. I listen to the nudge and it leads the way with a life of its own. I wasn't planning for it but it found its way into being."

This year, Maria adopted the cutest, sweetest kitten. She expected the adoption process to take longer than it did but was surprised. Maria found herself with the kitten effortlessly and easily. I could hear the delight in her voice over the phone when she told me that "it was love at first sight, and very magical."

Maria has been amazed by the way her word surprises her, every day. "Your word shows up in unexpected ways," she said. Maria recalled how she had called in Connection in December 2019 as her word for 2020. Little did she realize that she was about to embark on a journey that would lead to isolation for many in the midst of a global pandemic. Surprisingly, Maria ended up creating *richer* connections for herself during 2020. She became selective and only connected with those she felt a sense of a whole-body "yes! I want to spend some of my screen time with you!" Similarly with Magic, Maria had initially wanted a dramatic manifestation of this word but quickly realized how much more potent it was to notice the Magic in the everyday.

I asked Maria what she found most valuable about the practice of Call in Your Word. "It's a helpful way to stay focused on a particular intention," she said. "It's easy to remember one word for an entire year. The power of the Call in Your Word practice is in its simplicity."

BALANCE

"Things that challenge you in your work objectives are often things that you're lacking in your personal life. From a professional standpoint, having that intentionality or focus on a goal – like a word – is the piece that's missing from driving a whole individual. Bringing that human element into the workplace is essential."

When your dear friend, newly-appointed President and CEO of Elexicon Energy Inc., shatters the glass ceiling, you first rejoice and then proceed to pick her brain on her word for 2021, Balance.

Indrani embraced the practice of Call in Your Word with myself and amongst friends back in 2015. Little did she know what she was walking into that night. If you ask Indrani, she'll tell you that she showed up that night in the interest of gathering but had reservations about this new experience that I was proposing instead of our usual unstructured girls' night in.

"When you suggested we gather differently over this new practice, truthfully, it felt beyond my reach and beyond my comprehension as to why this would be of any value to me," Indrani said. "I'm used to goal setting professionally. It wasn't abundantly clear to me that this was something I was lacking in my life. If you're not missing it, you don't know you need it. I did think it was going to be a bit of bullshit because I didn't understand what value it had for me."

Not one to mince her words, Indrani was brutally honest. It's what I love most about her. I nudged her for more. What I really wanted to know was how this Type A woman, as Indrani calls herself, came to fall in love with the practice of calling in and living a word — a practice that's so different from setting goals and resolutions.

After a few years under her belt with this practice, Indrani reflected and told me. "Living a word is more important and more valuable than a resolution," she said. "A resolution suggests to me that you're going to change something, whereas a Word of the Year isn't necessarily about changing. It's about focus and that has a significantly different impact and energy for me. Change generally imparts that something was wrong, therefore, you need to change; whereas when you invite a Word of the Year, it's more about enhancement which suggests positivity. It's all about a positive evolution."

Did I mention Indrani knows a thing or two about leadership? Her willingness to open herself up to something new and to lead with curiosity was a treat for me to witness. "That's the beauty of embarking on something new," Indrani said. "Even if you embrace it half-heartedly, when you start to feel a word sitting in your subconscious, it's hard to avoid it. You may pay no focus to it but it's still subconsciously part of your approach. And so when I started to notice that my word was creating intersections within my personal, professional, and social lives, that's when I started to pay credence to it."

But here's what was really interesting for me to hear in the midst of my conversation with Indrani. As we chatted about the parallels and differences between the Call in Your Word practice and setting objectives/goals, and whether one is better than the other, she highlighted that setting objectives is about smart metrics. "It is measurable and time-bound," she said. "And once you achieve those metrics, only then are you considered 'successful.' I guess the Word of the Year is timebound, too, so it's not entirely different than setting goals and objectives but what I will say is that it's more fluid and that's the beauty of it. I'd love to layer on a word to an organizational framework. I bet my team would probably achieve greater success because of it. Things that challenge you in your work objective are often things that you're lacking in your personal life. From a professional standpoint, having that intentionality or focus on a goal -like a word- is the piece that is missing from driving a whole individual. Bringing that human element into the workplace is essential."

We both strongly agreed that when work cultures are sensitive to employees' values and internal motivators, outcomes related to productivity are more favorable. What better way to do that than through the power of a single word that speaks right to the person's overarching desire in all aspects of life?

Indrani called in Balance as her word for 2021 because she was feeling like she was compensating for all "the woes of Covid" by sitting at her desk for prolonged periods of time, trying to feel productive but the only thing she was actually productive at was being in front of the screen. Other aspects of her life were second to work and she was feeling negative instead.

At the beginning of 2021, Indrani became more intentional with Balance and started working out twice a day. One of those workouts would include her children which meant they were less on their devices and connecting more deeply with each other. Indrani was also heavily involved in recruitment and looking ahead towards an upward shift in her career. This move would signal a massive shift in all aspects of her life and not just in her profession.

The world changed in the middle of 2021 when restrictions were lifted, altering lifestyles once again. During this time, Indrani became more self-aware, self-compassionate, and patient, all of which she attributes to Balance. "Patience of and in itself is Balance. Impatience is frenetic and chaotic. Patience imparts opportunity to find balance, an opportunity to do the work that gets you to Balance," she said. "I probably wouldn't have gotten through this very chaotic middle had I not started off with a solid foundation with Balance. When launching into recruitment, you have to be vulnerable but from a grounded place. Without Balance by my side, I don't think I would've felt strong enough to work through this cycle of recruitment. Balance gave me strength."

Word of the Year

I asked Indrani who she would be without this practice. She responded, "I tend to be all in and extreme. Work is addictive. One thing about work is that it will take as many hours as you'll give it. It's funny that in this role as a CEO, people kept asking me- do you know what you're in for? I believe this is the opportunity for me, in my mid-40s with two young children, to be able to run an organization and still be there for my children. This is where Balance comes in again. It reminds me that I need to be better at setting boundaries. Balance is even more important in the tail end of this year and I believe I will achieve it."

KEEP GOING

"Call in Your Word is a personal, empowering, and nurturing practice that acts as an energetic tether, a faithful cheerleader, and a guiding light for helping you stay aligned to your truest self."

I've never met Kayla in person. She was my book coach as I was writing this tiny book (thank goodness for amazing book coaches!). Kayla is also an award-winning author and knows a thing or two about words. Kayla mentioned that she loves the Word of the Year practice and it's been a part of her life since 2007. Naturally, I gravitated towards her. I emailed her with such enthusiasm that I don't think she could say no to being interviewed. Excitement is contagious, my friends!

How did Kayla find this practice? Kayla shared with me that her inspiring older sister, Lacy, is friends with a group of well-known authors, artists, creatives, and leaders. When they all got together at a retreat to call in their words and then proceeded to paint their words on their bodies, Kayla was *captivated*.

For Kayla, the superpower of the Call in Your Word practice is intentionality. "I appreciate that it helps me practice focusing my intention and then giving that intention time to take root, grow and flourish," she said. "In an era of now, now, now, it's nice to have an intentional practice that is meant to take time to unfold. It also helps ground me through the year when I'm feeling lost or untethered. It reminds me of who I've been in clearer, stronger times, and it brings me back to my power and my focus. It's an energetic tether to my most aligned sense of self." Kayla's beautifully-described experience with this practice can be recreated anytime you call in your word, revisit your word, or call in a new word for a new phase or experience in your life.

How does Kayla formally engage in the process of calling in and living her word? "I start thinking about it in November/December and then begin to open my mind/heart to seeing/feeling what wants to find me," she told me. "I am an avid meditator and taught mysticism and meditation for many years, so my natural practice is to invite knowings during meditation. It's not a "formal" process for me. It looks different every year. Often there is journaling as well. But mostly it's meditation and a LOT of conversation with my big sis Lacy. If there happens to be a teacher I resonate with who is running a class, sometimes I'll jump into that. I've done a year-end review and new-year visioning sessions with Allison Crow, Rachel Brathen, my sister Lacy, and I've run my own for my clients in the past." Who doesn't love a good end of the year and New Year vision sessions? Raising my hand over here!

Once Kayla has called in her word, she journals about it at the beginning of the year and then reflects and meditates on her word throughout the year. She also connects with her sister and they engage in regular conversations about their words.

"We are constantly discussing how our words are or aren't showing themselves," she said. "It naturally stays top of mind for us."

In the past, Kayla has called in words like Express, Heal, Adelante, Promise, Grow, Me, Align, Focus, Soften, Write, Publish, and Wealth. "It's pretty cool to see how my life has pretty much followed that trend," Kayla said. "Grow is particularly memorable because I became unexpectedly pregnant that year, and I literally GREW a human. Also, I can see now in hindsight how much healing and self-discovery needed to happen before I could get to the writing, publishing, and success I was craving all those years ago."

When Kayla called in a word for 2021, she initially called in Success and Health. I laughed when I read what she had to say right after this: "I went all rogue this year and chose two!" But as often as it happens in this practice, we achieve Success and Health when we remain flexible and allow life to inspire, or change, our chosen word. Kayla shifted her word when she needed to.

Words Invite Magic

It's no secret that my favorite experience about having a Word of the Year is the synchronicities that come along for the ride. This has been the case for many. These countless synchronicities support our dreams and infuse magic into the ordinary. We've all been blown away by the fact that our words have shown up everywhere and propelled us forward simply by being visible and audible.

Words Build Connection

I can't even begin to tell you how often I'm told that when we share our words, conversations take enchanting twists and turns towards vulnerability and depth in a way that no "small talk" ever can. Oftentimes, we also find ourselves in each other's words and in the richness of these stories (hence this book!). This level of engagement is exactly what's been happening in my Live Your Word community, too. To be witnessed and heard with your word as a vehicle and as a gateway into the true parts of yourself is

"In February I faced some struggles, and I felt those words shift into 'Keep Going.' Success and Health are still my intentions, but the words I cling to now and repeat to myself often for this year are 'Keep Going.' They feel like faithful friends and cheerleaders, and they've served me to manage the ups and downs of life. When I feel lost or am struggling, the words 'keep going' is there to scoot me along to the next small loving step I can take. It feels like my most potent year yet."

Without the practice of Call in Your Word, Kayla might have missed out on a larger vision. "I don't think I'd be as great at seeing the big picture in my life," she said. "It's so easy to get mired in the day-to-day stress of life. The year-long commitment to a word has helped me be a bigger picture person who understands that small steps consistently over time lead to big results (thanks to Alex and Linds for driving home that one as well!). I see my life through a different lens, and I am also better at remembering my immense power when I feel small or unsteady." Massive kudos to that!

Kayla wants you to experience the power of this practice. "Call in Your Word is a personal, empowering, and nurturing practice that acts as an energetic tether, a faithful cheerleader, and a guiding light for helping you stay aligned to your truest self."

WORDS AS TRUTH

As I continue to deepen my r[elationship] with my words, I've uncove[red] truths about this practice al[ong the] way. Dare I say you've probably n[oticed] some of the truths embedded wit[hin the] pages of this book in your own lif[e?] Nicole's story of Slow was the ge[ntle] permission you needed to invite i[n? Or] was it Mira's word, Open, that all[owed] the sweet surrender and acceptan[ce you've] been waiting for? Can it be that w[ords like] Delight and Devoted will help you [find] abundance in your life as they did [for Anna] and Stephanie?

As you begin to sync with your ow[n] rhythms and weave your way into [the] divinity of your words, your truth[s will] undoubtedly surface. Until then, h[ere's] what I know about how words unr[avel in] us and *for* us:

such a healing and transformative experience.

Words Know Best

One of the first things I noticed about the Call in Your Word practice is that while you may have specific intentions for your word, your word will show up for you in a way you need it most and not always as you desired. *Guaranteed!*

Think of your word as a wise friend. You'd want your friend to be honest and truthful and personally, I can do without the sugar coating. Similarly, your word is here to serve you with what you need most and may not even know it. In an ideal world, we'd be able to do that for ourselves but when you need that gentle push to exercise self-compassion, to set up stronger boundaries, to rest...y'know, all the things that are likely at the bottom of our to-do lists, your word is here to ensure that you look after *you*.

Words Attract Opposites/Shadows

When we call in a word, we also call in its opposite. In other words, a word also carries with it a shadow.

Opposites and shadows offer us alternative views, new ideas, and an invitation to lean into our edges. While I love how fun and easy calling in and living our words can be, the truth is that this practice runs deep. Both can co-exist and herein lies the beauty of this practice. Digging deep into the mystery of the word and its hidden meanings adds an element of mysticism to the practice.

Words Provide Anchoring

I've lost count of how many times I've heard "anchor" come up in my conversations when I was writing this book. Oftentimes, we look to our word as our North Star, guiding light, an anchor to the ground that roots us. That's exactly it! These single words carry with them such phenomenal strength in their ability to provide us with anchoring in the moments we need them the most.

Words Create Clarity + Ease

If called in with intention, our words ultimately connect us to our values and purpose. Whether I'm calling in my word or facilitating others to call in theirs, I spend quite a bit of time exploring the recent past to create the future. Much of this process is rooted in re-connecting with our values and our purpose to map out a clear road ahead.

It's no wonder that our words symbolize our deepest longings with ease and clarity because we've called them in with such conviction.

Words Strengthen Intuition

You've heard this before: we're all intuitive beings. I love how our words have the ability to return us back to ourselves and in doing so, connect us with our wisest and highest selves. This is the birthplace of intuition. Strengthening our intuition requires regular practice and I, for one, am loving using my word as a tool to do exactly that.

In my seven years of this practice, I've noticed these universal elements of trust and assurance with those who are living their lives, one word at a time.

READER REFLECTIONS

Having soaked in all the magnificence of these stories of single words with massive impact, I'd like to invite you to reflect on what this practice might have to offer you. Use the following pages to answer prompts about your inspirations, values, and future goals.

Reflecting back on your life, what has your relationship been with goals, habits, objectives, etc.? What's worked and what hasn't?

_____

_____

_____

_____

_____

_____

_____

_____

Word of the Year

What story from this book was your favorite and why?

_____

_____

_____

_____

_____

_____

_____

_____

_____

_____

Word of the Year

Where in your life could you see the Call in Your Word practice be of value?

Word of the Year

Which one of the Word Truths resonated the most with you? Elaborate.

_____

_____

_____

_____

_____

_____

_____

_____

_____

_____

Word of the Year

Imagine for a moment that you called in a word. How would you build your relationship with it? What nourishing rituals would you create to forward momentum with your word?

_____

_____

_____

_____

_____

_____

_____

_____

Word of the Year

Looking ahead, if you engaged in the Call in Your Word practice, how would your life be different 3, 6, or 12 months from now?

Word of the Year

Will you commit to choosing a word this year? What hesitations do you have? What's exciting to you about the Call in Your Word practice?

_____

_____

_____

_____

_____

_____

_____

_____

_____

_____

Word of the Year

If you're looking for more guidance with the Call in Your Word practice, look no further! I love helping people like you Call in Your Word and have created a number of resources and tools that you can choose from to support you on this journey. I would suggest checking out my self-paced online [Call in Your Word program](#) to start. dimplemukherjee.teachable.com

If you're still curious, sign up for my monthly newsletter where I share regular tips on calling in and living your word. dimplemukherjee.com

Once you have called in your word, don't stop there. The [Live Your Word journal](#) is a free downloadable guide to help you strengthen your relationship with your word and its presence in your life. This journal is filled with monthly inspirations, reflection prompts, and action steps that will motivate you to move forward in a way that feels fulfilling and nourishing. dimplemukherjee.com/liveyourword

Lastly, if you want to go all out and connect with others who are a big fan of this practice, consider joining the [Live Your Word community](#) — an online space where we meet monthly to connect over our words and it's a real treat to come together in this way. dimplemukherjee.com/community

These are just a few ways to build momentum in your life with your word and I hope you will take full advantage of them. The real fun is in the connection: your connection with your word and your connection with other people and their words with your word by your side.

CLOSING

The web of words. An interesting concept in and of itself. From the time we're born, our caregivers eagerly await our first words. Typically, no more than a bunch of sounds weaved together, we make of it what we want. We exchange words simply to be witnessed and heard. Words to ease pain and suffering, words to fill the void, words to manifest desires, words to retaliate, words to self soothe or comfort, words to shed anger, words to hold in silence and the list goes on. So many choices and options to do what we want with our words and at a whim but rarely do we make meaning of the privilege in these words.

Now think back to all the times when your words escaped you in the most inopportune of times? Or moments when you silenced your words and regretted doing so? How would your words have been received?

Consider this: *our words carry weight*. This phrase is often utilized and widely shared. Our words have an impact. And in the midst of all of our words is an interconnectedness.

A thread that ties my word to yours and yours to mine and to the next and so on. The magnification of your word is only as good as your willingness to share it, to have someone witness it, and to allow another into the depth of your word and your world. The otherness and the oneness of our words – the way in which we find ourselves in each other's words and stay there - is the beauty of the Call in Your Word practice.

GRATITUDE

Writing a book truly takes a village! Tremendous thanks to the souls who generously donated their time and hearts to this book project. Quite literally, I couldn't have done it without all of you:

Stephanie Pellett, Creative Support & Consulting, stephaniepellett.com

Sonja Seiler, founder of Nurture, nurtureretreats.com

Julia

Georgia Reynolds, Team Coach, georgiareynolds.ca

R.G., Clinical Counsellor

Mira

Nicole Kagan, Visual Artist and Creative Mindfulness Facilitator, nicolekagan.com

Word of the Year

Maria Ramsey, founder of [The Philosopher's Stem](), thephilosophersstem.com

Indrani Butany-DeSouza, President and CEO of Elexicon Energy Inc.

Kayla Floyd, Award-Winning Author of ["*Joyful Mornings: Mindful Poems for Inviting Happy Days*" and "*Wondrous You: Empowering Poems for Magical Kids*"](), kaylafloyd.com

I also need to say thank you to...

[Firefly Creative Writing]() for igniting the fire in my belly that I never knew existed and granting me the permission to call myself a writer. Special thanks to Chris and Britt- writers and coaches extraordinaire. fireflycreativewriting.com

The brilliant and vibrant team at the [Tiny Book Course]() for being my cheerleaders during this leg of my writing journey as an author of a tiny book. tinybookcourse.com

The creative humans of my business mastermind group, [The Profoundery](), and my business coach, Stephanie, for encouraging me to share my unique gifts with the world. stephaniepellett.com

All my clients, newsletter subscribers, and blog readers who have been following my work over the years and watching it evolve. Thank you for trusting me and I'm grateful for your presence in my life.

My friends for being open to that night back in December 2015 when we called in our words of the year as a group for the first time ever!

Mala – thank you for being my number one supporter from day one! You've been my sounding board and confidante through all of the highs and lows. So grateful for you.

My beloved family – my parents, siblings and their spouses, nieces and nephews, partner, ex-husband, sister in law, and in-laws. When you look after my boys and feed me, I'm able to tend to my writing. Thank you for nourishing and loving me. I love you all so much.

Ramu- for shaping me into who I am today. I'll forever be blessed by your presence in my life.

Virginia-my 18-year-old cat who made her way into my life at the tender age of 2 months. She knew I needed a cat even when I didn't. How did I get SO lucky with you?

Aavik, Ishaan, and Aaryn – my three tender beings and inspiration for everything. Thank you for choosing me as your mother. Little did I know you would become my wisest teachers.

Approximately one million other people that I am forgetting right now. Thank you. Everyone.

ABOUT THE AUTHOR

Dimple Mukherjee is an Occupational Therapist, Word Coach, the co-author of two books – Inspired Living and Women Rising (Volume 3) – and an herbalist in training. Her life philosophy is rooted in and centered around good health and wellness. Dimple has dedicated the past few years to learning and understanding how profoundly words can shape our lives and improve our mental health.

Dimple lives in Toronto with her three sons and a geriatric cat (who also happens to be the love of her life) and hoards books like they're going out of fashion.

Find Dimple's programs, workshops, and coaching here: www.dimplemukherjee.com

www.ingramcontent.com/pod-product-compliance
Lightning Source LLC
Chambersburg PA
CBHW011318080526
44589CB00020B/2746